HOW THE
SEVEN
WONDERS
OF THE ANCIENT WORLD
WERE BUILT

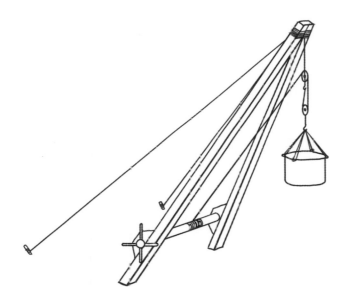

Albatros

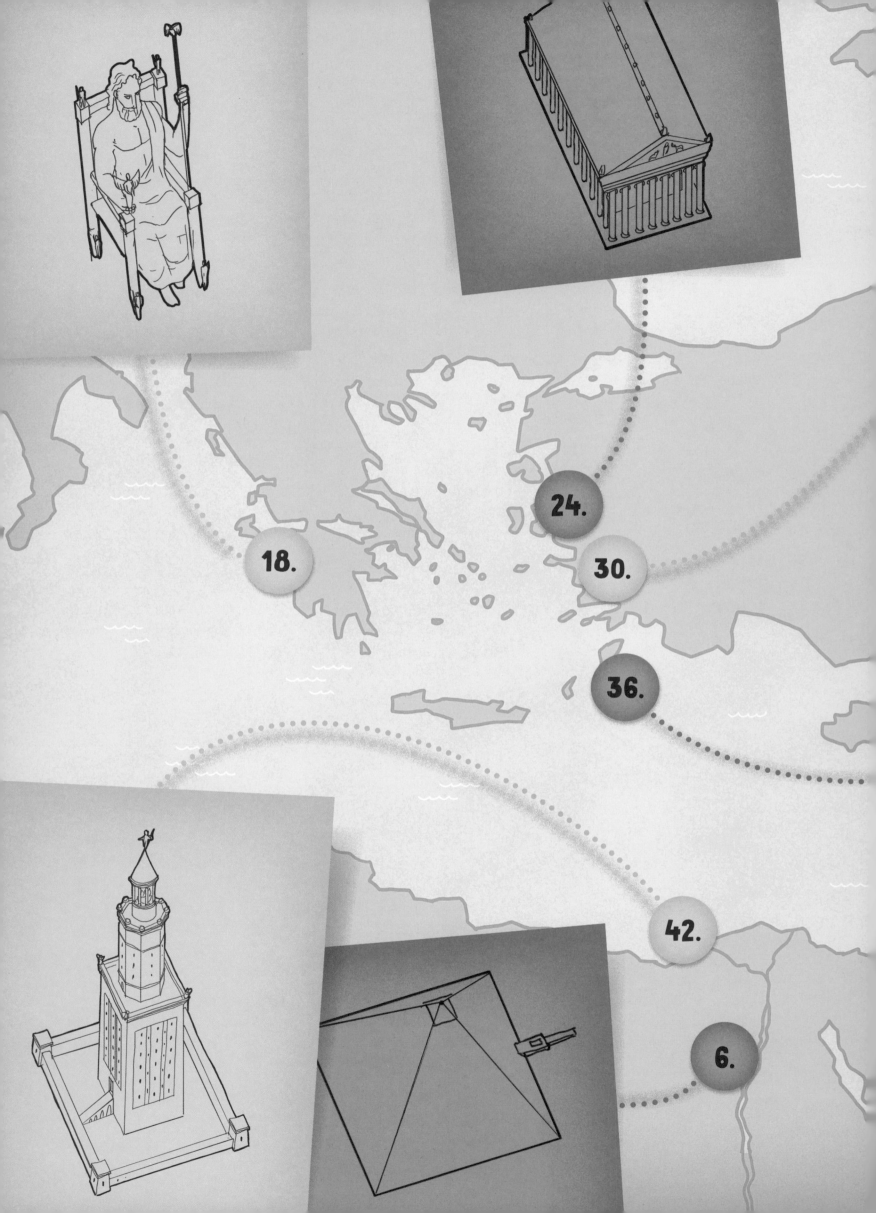

Content

12.

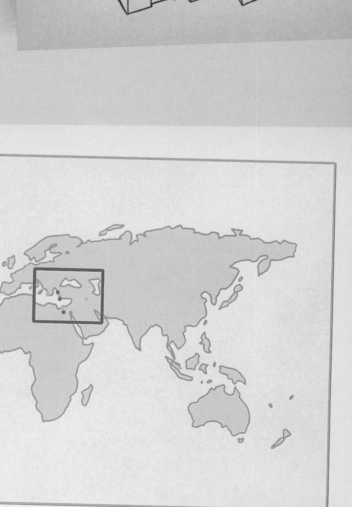

Introduction

....

They shine from the past ... and their light is undiminished. The gems of antiquity are proof that humans can compete with the wonders of nature. People have always wanted more: to improve existing methods and find new opportunities. They want to create something new, something that evokes a feeling of amazement and admiration. A masterpiece that will make their creators famous during their lifetimes and immortal thereafter.

From the inconspicuous to the gigantic

All masterpieces begin with a first small step. An idea. A plan. A drawing. Before building a pyramid, a giant statue, or a hanging garden, it takes millions of small steps, small strenuous activities, daily work, and blood, sweat, and tears to realize the vision that the author wanted to give dimension, color, and shape to. Fascinating, isn't it?

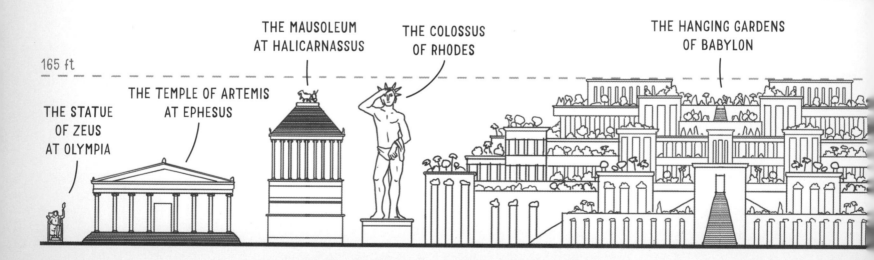

165 ft

THE STATUE OF ZEUS AT OLYMPIA

THE TEMPLE OF ARTEMIS AT EPHESUS

THE MAUSOLEUM AT HALICARNASSUS

THE COLOSSUS OF RHODES

THE HANGING GARDENS OF BABYLON

The Seven Wonders of the World

The list of the Wonders of the World has evolved over the years. After all, their nascency covers a long historical period from the third millennium BC, when the oldest and only preserved Egyptian pyramids were built, to the first millennium BC, when other buildings saw the light of day. The travelers and writers of the world were certainly not lazy. They wandered long distances across countries, most often by sea, to find and report to everyone about a breathtaking colossus, a lighthouse, some gardens, and other marvels. And where else should the list come from than the cultural center of Egypt—Alexandria. And why seven? Well, there are seven days in the week, seven sacraments, and seven virtues. In the Middle Ages, there were even seven liberal arts. The number seven denotes completeness and mysticism—what do you think?

Myth or reality?

Nowadays we can do many things, like talk to people from the other side of the world, sink to the bottom of the ocean, or launch into space. But we still can't go back in time. Fortunately, there are historians and archeologists who want to know what it looked like in the past and how people without modern technology could build such colossal structures. Their opinions differ and we do not know for sure how it all was. But we can believe them and delve into the sometimes unbelievable stories of "How the Seven Wonders of the Ancient World Were Built."

SIZE COMPARISON OF THE WONDERS WITH THE EIFFEL TOWER

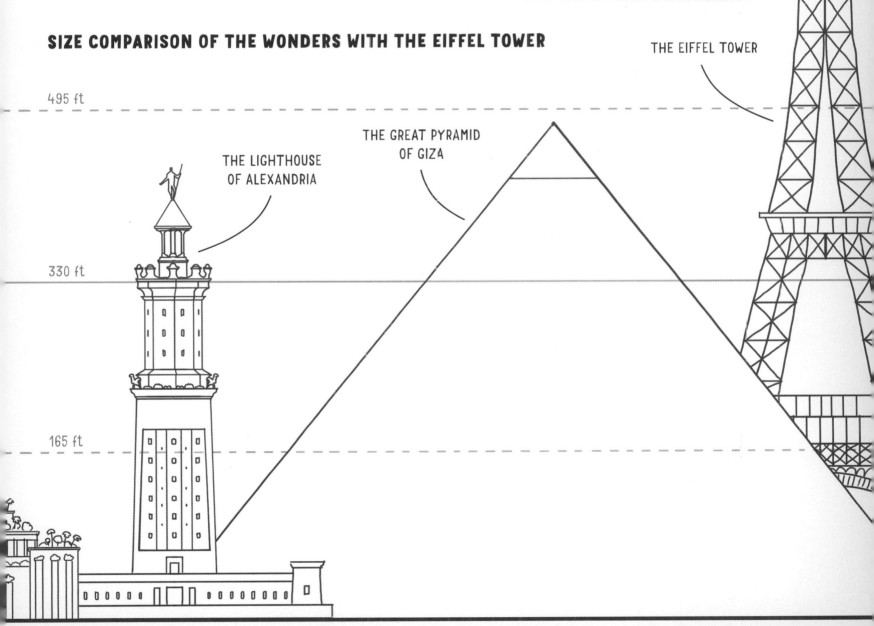

495 ft

THE EIFFEL TOWER

THE LIGHTHOUSE OF ALEXANDRIA

THE GREAT PYRAMID OF GIZA

330 ft

165 ft

The Pyramids of Giza

This is the only wonder that has survived thousands of years of sun, wind, and the ravages of time. The Pyramids of Egypt were built during the Fourth Dynasty in the third millennium BC. They consist of the Great Pyramid of Giza (also known as the Pyramid of Khufu or of Cheops), the Pyramid of Khafre, and the Pyramid of Menkaure. Many questions regarding their construction have not been—and probably will never be—answered. That's why this text is interspersed with words like *probably, possibly, or likely*. Anyways, let's dive into the mystery!

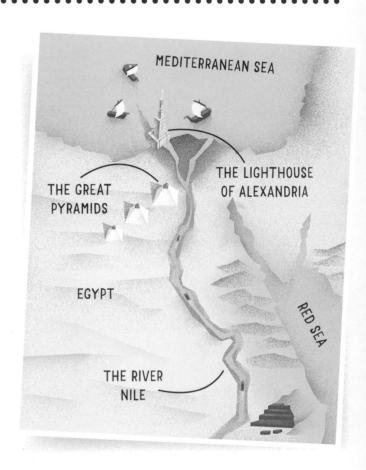

MEDITERRANEAN SEA

THE LIGHTHOUSE OF ALEXANDRIA

THE GREAT PYRAMIDS

EGYPT

RED SEA

THE RIVER NILE

The greatest of them all

The Great Pyramid of Giza, also known as the Pyramid of Khufu, is the largest, most beautiful, and best preserved of the three pyramids. Its walls face the four cardinal points—north, south, east, and west—and each has a base of more than 750 feet. It weighs about 5 million tons, standing at 450 feet. It was originally at least 30 feet higher, but over the centuries, it lost its decorative top. At the time of construction, it was covered with limestone cladding because each pyramid of Ancient Egypt was supposed to shine and sparkle in the sun. Today, the cladding can only be found at the top.

Land on the Nile

Pharaoh Khufu chose the plateau of Giza to be his resting place, as it provided sufficiently strong bedrock for the construction of such a grand monument. The location was also advantageous because of the nearby Nile, a great traffic artery. The river was used to transport limestone from the town of Tora and granite from the Aswan quarries, which were located more than 500 miles to the south. Can't you just hear the waves breaking against the ships?

PYRAMID OF KHAFRE

PYRAMID OF MENKAURE

PYRAMIDS OF QUEENS

THE PHARAOH WAS ESSENTIALLY A GOD

The Pharaoh's architect

"Here, your majesty, will stand a pyramid rising into the sky. A perfect square, look, your royal highness!" the architect welcomed his cousin, Pharaoh Khufu. He visited the site several times to check on the progress of his resting place. In addition to the pyramid, the tomb complex included a valley temple, a causeway, and a mortuary temple. All the parts were designed and planned together, but the pyramid was the top priority. It was measured and constructed first. The architect couldn't afford to make any mistakes!

Khufu's crafty family

We don't know much about Pharaoh Khufu, but preserved papyri depict him as a cruel and despotic ruler. He was the son of King Sneferu and Queen Hetepheres I. He had enormous power, enforced absolutism, and owned all the land in the kingdom and every subject in it. The title of the greatest pharaoh of Ancient Egypt is also based on his architectural achievements, including the Great Pyramid and the surrounding temple complex. He was the only one who managed to build such a monumental pyramid, although many others tried, including his son Khafre and his grandson Menkaure.

Pyramid cross-section

The entrance of the pyramid was accessed by a down-sloping passage that led to the oldest burial chamber. Later, the passages leading from the original entrance went upwards. At a height of over a hundred feet above the bedrock, there is a middle space designated as the Queen's Chamber. The largest space in each pyramid was the internal gallery. This one is 150 feet long and 27 feet high and leads to the highest King's Chamber, which served as the resting place of Pharaoh Khufu. The third chamber is located halfway up the pyramid.

PHARAOH KHUFU

PYRAMID OF GIZA

On the site

The Pyramid of Khufu was probably built around 2550 BC and has been guarding a great secret for several millennia. How could they build such a massive monument when they didn't have pulleys, iron, or other more complex tools?

Ramps

The pyramid grew thanks to work ramps. One led from the pier and canal, where construction materials and supplies for workers were transported on ships. The second one most likely led from a quarry near the pyramid, from which a number of the stone blocks were imported. To a certain height, two straight ramps with a slight slope were used; in higher positions, there was a spiral inner ramp around the structure. Unfortunately, the Great Pyramid itself doesn't provide any evidence, so we only have the speculations of historians.

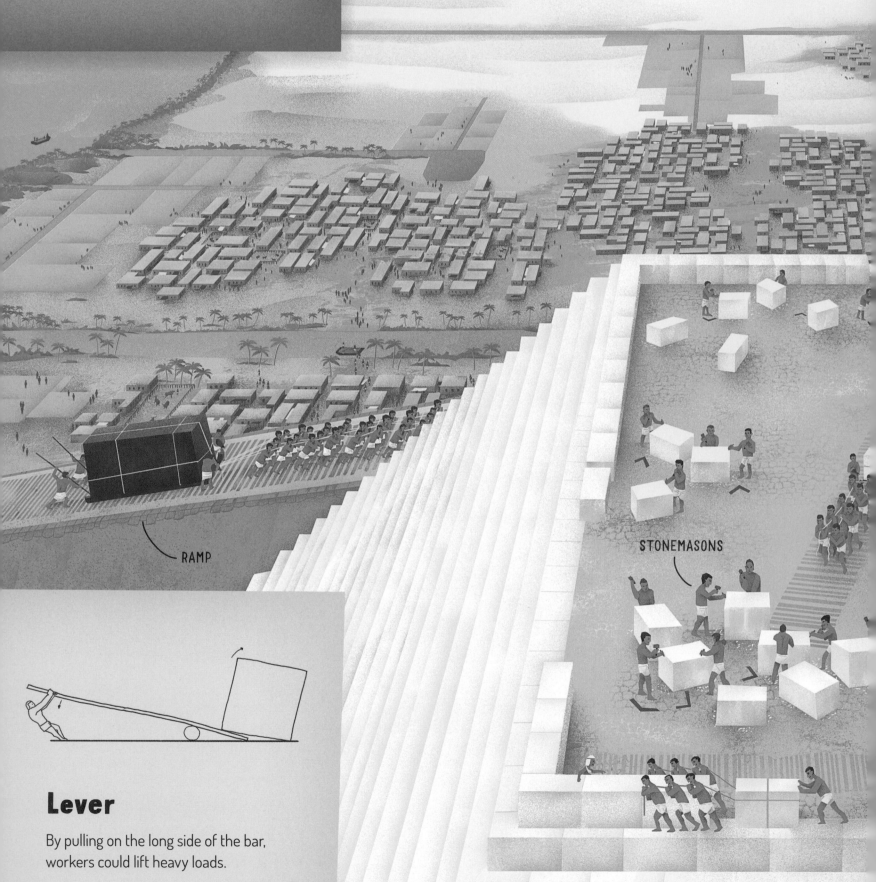

RAMP

STONEMASONS

Lever

By pulling on the long side of the bar, workers could lift heavy loads.

A town of workers

Over 20 years, the construction of the pyramids employed around 20,000 skilled artisans and free peasants—not slaves, as historians once thought. Stonemasons had a privileged position. A workers' town made of unfired bricks has been found near the structures. It included bakeries, fish shops, water mills, and windmills. Hardworking artisans were well provided for.

Material

The Great Pyramid of Giza was built on bedrock to ensure a solid foundation for this magnificent structure. The core of the pyramid consists of hard and resistant granite, and the surface was originally covered with Tora limestone, which made the pyramid shine. The limestone casing was attached to granite blocks for stability, and it was all hewn and polished. When construction ended, the ramps were then taken down.

QUARRY

WORKERS' TOWN

RAMP

WORKERS PUSHING A BLOCK

Let it slide

One stone block weighed over 2 tons, and nearly 3 million of them were used in the construction. They were shifted using ropes, levers, round tree trunks, and enormous manpower. Water was poured in front of them to lessen the friction. The stones were thus covered with a thin layer of mud, which made the work easier. Wooden sleds were also very useful.

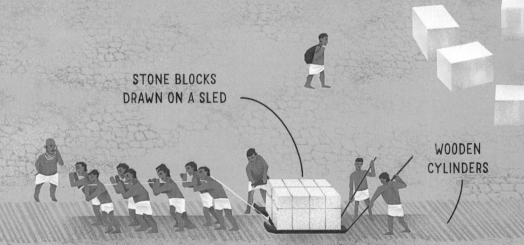

STONE BLOCKS DRAWN ON A SLED

WOODEN CYLINDERS

Predecessors of the pyramids

Afterlife palaces were first carved into rocks. They were later extended by a superstructure called a mastaba, which was made of fired bricks, and occasionally stone. It was the direct predecessor of the pyramids and was used to store funerary offerings for the deceased; wealthy people ever had several rooms in there. Imhotep, a philosopher, physician, poet, and court architect of Pharaoh Djoser, came up with the idea to pile up several mastabas, thus creating the pyramid in Saqqara, the first of its kind. Pyramids became very popular at that time, and every ruler wanted to have one.

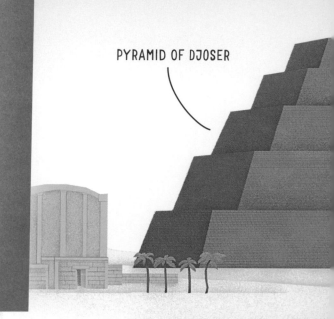

PYRAMID OF DJOSER

Afloat

Preparing stone blocks in the quarry was a strenuous task. That's why the work was only entrusted to the most skilled stonemasons and craftsmen. Once the granite and limestone blocks were ready, they had to be transported as close to the pyramid as possible. The best method—as documented in recently discovered papyri—was to transport them by water, as the workers could use the Nile and the dense network of canals leading to each pyramid, if the subsoil allowed it.

TRANSPORT SHIP

A master stonemason's work

Hard granite blocks were made by disturbing the rock surface using fire and water in turns. They then made gouges with copper chisels, drove hardwood wedges into them, and poured water onto the wedges. The expanding wood either broke the stone itself or made it possible to break it using crowbars. Broken-off granite blocks were then attached to a platform and further worked with a copper saw pulled by several men on each side. They used a kind of sand called silica sand as the abrasive material.

It holds together!

The blocks didn't always have a perfect shape. Well, even experts make mistakes sometimes. We know that the granite blocks in the core were crafted poorly and roughly, and the gaps between them were filled with plaster mortar. Mortar was also used to attach the limestone cladding. Final adjustments and hewing away excess cladding required wooden scaffolding. Occupational safety had to be observed even in Ancient Egypt.

PLASTER MORTAR

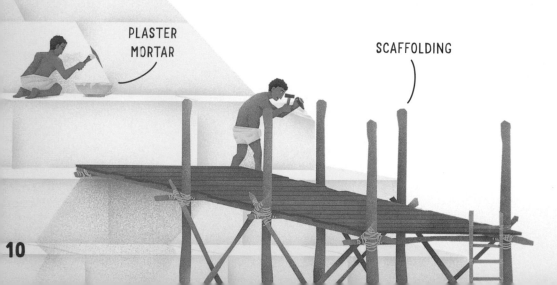

SCAFFOLDING

The afterlife

In Ancient Egypt, rulers and important members of their families were buried in tombs. Sumptuous dwellings and true afterlife palaces were built for the deceased so that they had space for their soul. As they saw it back then, the soul could only survive if the remains were present in this world. That was ensured by the mummification process, which started immediately after death and could last more than 70 days. At the very end, the corpse was wrapped in a cloth along with various amulets and magic formulas.

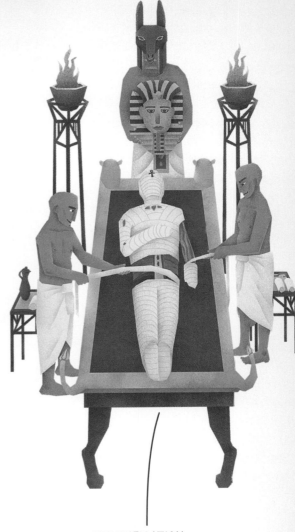

MUMMIFICATION PROCESS

Sun boats

When all the steps of the mummification process were completed, the corpse could then be buried in the tomb. The ruler's embalmed body was transported on the Nile by a special ship called a sun boat directly to the mortuary temple, where glorious ceremonies and celebrations could begin. In the mid-20th century, Egyptian archeologists made a rare discovery. In the Great Pyramid, they found Khufu's sun boat dismantled into individual parts, and they managed to assemble it once again over ten years!

SUN BOAT

Khufu's legacy

The mysteries and size of the Pyramids of Giza strike people speechless with wonder. The Great Pyramid of Giza has been admired by visitors to Egypt for over 4,500 years. Despite numerous rumors, assumptions, theories, and hypotheses, we still cannot say exactly how the pyramids were built. And who knows if this mystery will ever be cracked.

COMPARISON WITH THE EIFFEL TOWER

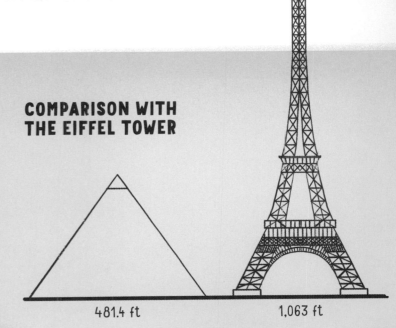

481.4 ft   1,063 ft

The Hanging Gardens of Babylon

None of the Wonders of the World were as mysterious as this one. Did they exist or not? God—perhaps an Ancient Greek or Roman one—only knows. Either way, they looked like they were hanging in the air and were formed by a series of pyramid-like arcade terraces. Their peak seemed to be invisible in the distance. Tree branches waved and a flowery mist rose to the sky—an image of paradise. Exotic trees with enormous roots, flowers of various colors, and grasses and plants of unparalleled beauty.

Welcome to Babylon!

The Babylonian Empire was powerful and impressive. This gigantic state of the Near East thrived in the 6th century BCE, ruled by Nebuchadnezzar II, who was devoted to his love, Princess Amytis. The queen, Semiramis, is a historical figure steeped in myth and legend, whose name is associated with the gardens. The construction of the Hanging Gardens is attributable to the real Amytis, who grew up in the mountains of Media and yearned for the wild beauty of nature in the royal palace. Let's face it, there's nothing some people won't do for love! Why not build an artificial mountain, for example?

A solid foundation is essential

The most important part of any structure is the foundation. This is unsurprising since the gardens were reportedly 400 feet long on each side. Imagine majestic terraces, vaults, arches, arcades, and countless stairs that could take you to the very top overlooking the mountains.

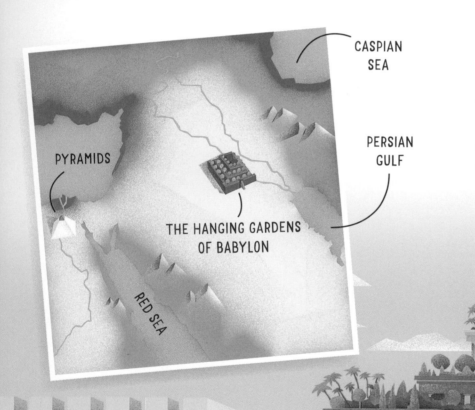

CASPIAN SEA

PERSIAN GULF

PYRAMIDS

THE HANGING GARDENS OF BABYLON

RED SEA

Secrets of the garden

Along the way, you pass paths lined with flower beds filled with tons of soil, stunning flowers, and full-grown trees. You also encounter various water attractions. Surrounding the staircases are ancient machines called Archimedean screws, which pump water upward from the Euphrates. According to some sources, the Hanging Gardens were presented as numerous terraces resembling mountains.

A builder of paradise

Nebuchadnezzar II made his mark as the biblical king who besieged Jerusalem, destroyed the Kingdom of Judah, and caused the Babylonian captivity of the Jews. During his reign, he managed to form the most powerful empire, bringing fame to the capital city of Babylon due to the many structures built by the best engineers and builders. The Hanging Gardens of Babylon are one of them. They became part of the king's palace, where Nebuchadnezzar and Amytis could enjoy this paradise on earth admired far and wide.

THE GREENERY RESEMBLED THE BIRTHPLACE OF AMYTIS

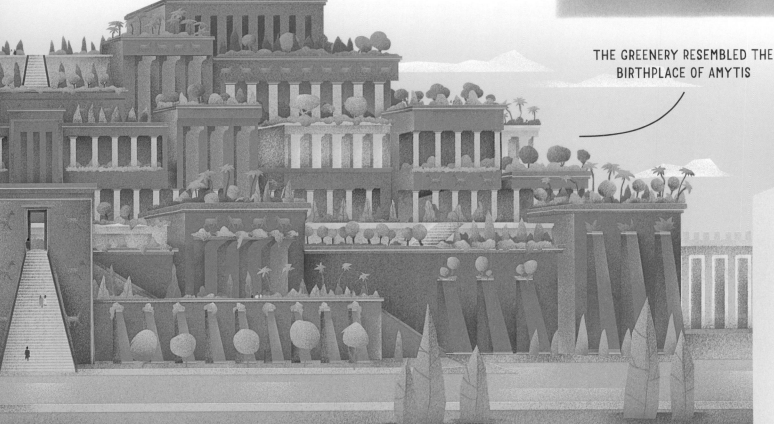

Unlimited working hours!

Those who expected to find peace after the construction was completed were disappointed. Once everything was finished, the gardens had to be maintained. And again, that required a great deal of working staff. But what did they do? Fertilizing, aerating, planting, weeding, maintaining, grassing, mowing, cutting, shortening, breaking . . . We know about all that. The most demanding task, however, was irrigation.

Archimedean screw

By turning the screw of this ancient machine, the builders were able to take up water and irrigate hard-to-reach places at higher elevations.

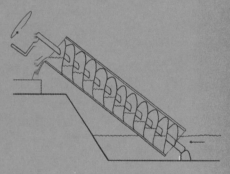

Bricks

Bricks were needed the most. Why? Because Babylon was located in an area with a lack of stone and wood. Stone was imported and only used in exceptional cases for selected structures. Fired and unfired bricks were used the most in the city's construction industry. Unfired bricks, which were hollow and filled with clay, were used to build the foundations. Fired bricks were used as cladding and at stress points.

Get to work!

The construction of the Hanging Gardens required enormous human resources. Fortunately for the king—and unfortunately for his captives—Nebuchadnezzar had many slaves whom he had enslaved during his many conquests. Thousands of people worked on the construction, including slaves, architects, engineers, builders, material carriers—who mainly transported huge volumes of soil, as well as plants and exotic trees—and brick manufacturers.

Asphalt and mortar

To make the construction solid, workers reinforced the bricks with clay mortar and asphalt, often adding plaster to the mortar. Where the joints had to be sealed, lead was poured over the bricks. Asphalt and feldspar, also called bitumen, were often used as well.

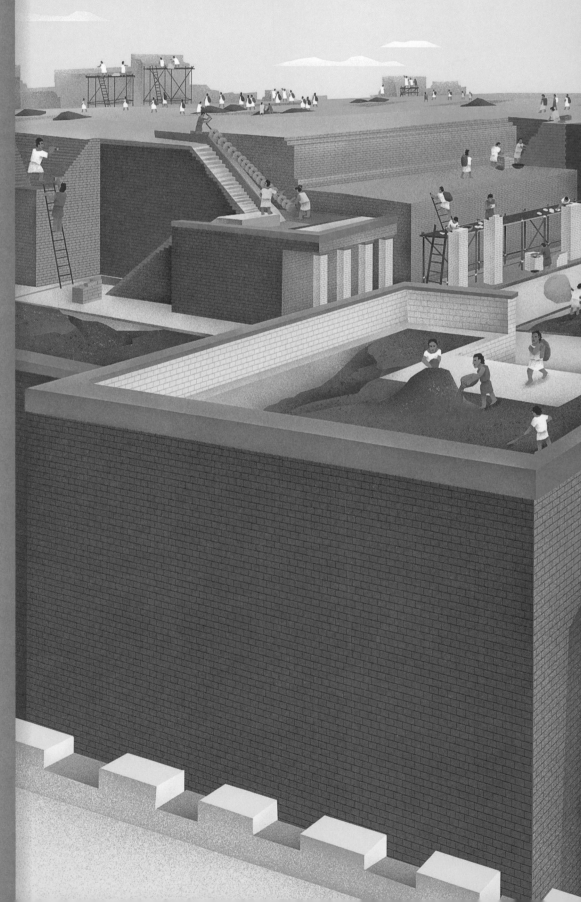

Ishtar's lion

The city was surrounded by walls accessible through gates. The most famous one is the Ishtar Gate. Its corner was adjacent to the royal palace. It was lavishly decorated with symbols of gods. There were mighty dragons, symbols of the god Marduk, as well as large bulls celebrating the god of thunderstorms (Adad) and, above all, symbols of the goddess Ishtar: noble lions.

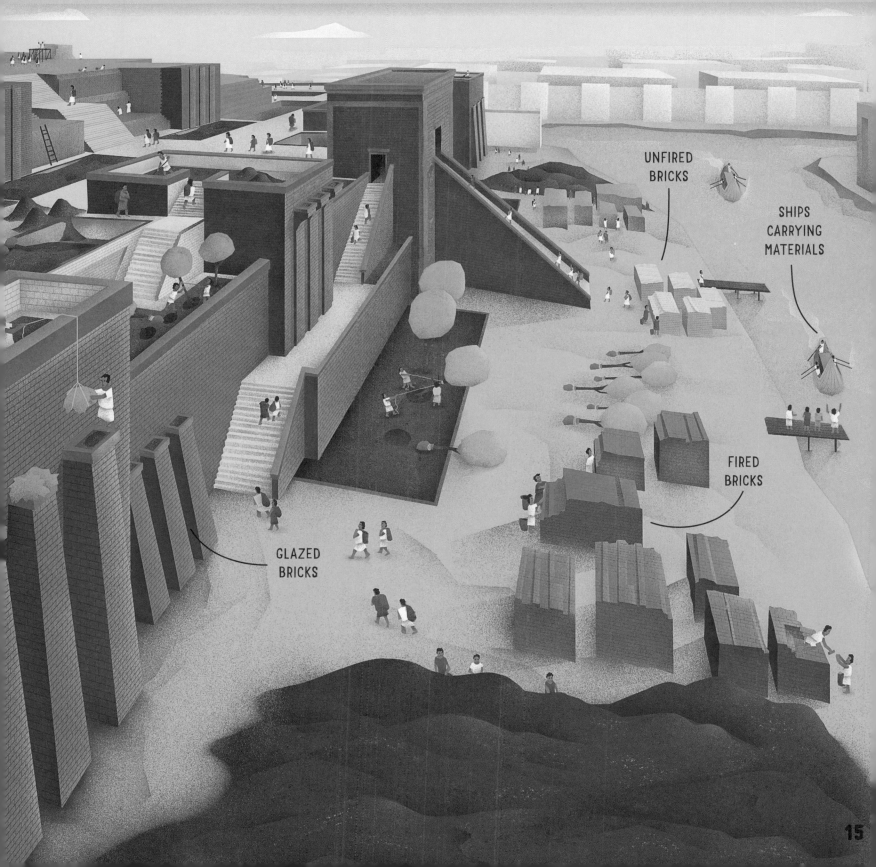

UNFIRED BRICKS

SHIPS CARRYING MATERIALS

FIRED BRICKS

GLAZED BRICKS

Gardens

At the time of the Babylonian Empire, gardens were a symbol of luxury. Rulers who wanted to have some rest or declare their love used flowers, trees, and plants to form a paradise on earth in which they felt like gods. Who wouldn't like that? However, the gardens were also located in the city. They offered space for rest and shelter from the scorching sun. There were also orchards with trees bearing delicious and tempting fruit. Stories associated with gardens can be found in ancient epic poems, such as the *Epic of Gilgamesh*.

ARCHIMEDEAN SCREW

Water? Water!!!

A lot of water was needed to irrigate such huge gardens. But how to get it where it is needed? Fortunately, the life-giving Euphrates was bubbling nearby and waterways could be used. This river brought water through canals to the gardens, where it was stored in tanks and flowed to the individual floors by means of spiral pumps called Archimedean screws. Each floor had a water tank from which the water was pumped by another screw to the next floor, all the way up to the top, where the water then flowed down to nourish the plants.

Hesitation

The historical sources on the Hanging Gardens of Babylon have never been definitively confirmed. Even the celebrated "Father of History," Herodotus, who lived in the 5th century BCE, did not describe the gardens after visiting Babylon, although he mentioned all the other buildings. Archeologists have also tried their best to substantiate the existence of the Hanging Gardens based on excavations, but to date they have been unsuccessful.

Tower & walls

Almost everything in Babylon could be classified as a wonder of the ancient world. Besides the gardens, there was the Tower of Babel, which had a temple and an astronomical observatory at the top, as well as the Babylonian walls. Some sources say that the walls were so wide that a four-horse chariot could ride atop it.

Truth or fiction?

The German archeologist Robert Koldewey discovered a complex that he considered the Gardens of Babylon, as well as clay tablets with records of oil and barley rations. He did not maintain his enthusiasm, however, for very long. His interpretation was disproved by later research, which demonstrated that the complex was actually the remains of an elevated path. The tablet as an artifact of the Hanging Garden was problematic, as it was discovered quite far from the Euphrates.

The Statue of Zeus at Olympia

The Statue of Zeus at Olympia was said to have enchanted everyone who saw it. That's not at all surprising. With its colossal height of 40 feet, it had to have looked spectacular in the temple. If it were to come to life and stand up, its head would have broken through the roof. The god Zeus, with his long hair and beard, sat atop a black block pedestal on a beautiful cedar throne. His chest was partially covered by a gilded robe, made from then-precious glass and carved with lilies.

OLYMPIA

MEDITERRANEAN SE

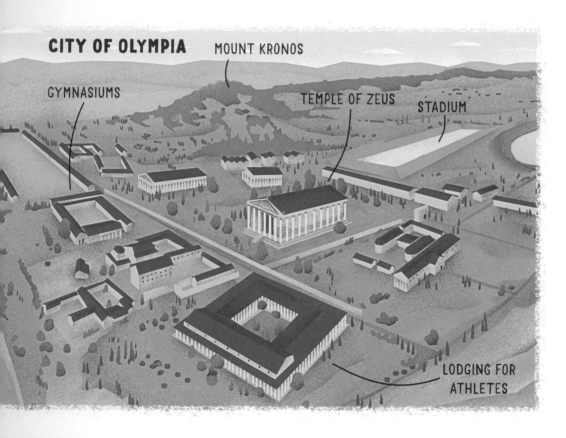

CITY OF OLYMPIA
MOUNT KRONOS
GYMNASIUMS
TEMPLE OF ZEUS
STADIUM
LODGING FOR ATHLETES

The greatest god, the greatest temple

Olympia was one of the most important city-states of the powerful Ancient Greek Empire. In its center, the largest temple on the Peloponnese peninsula was built to celebrate the victory in the Greco-Persian wars. Ceremonies were held at the temple to honor Zeus, which probably evolved into the Olympic Games, the first of which took place in 776 BCE and were held every four years.

A god made of gold & ivory

In his outstretched right hand he held a winged statue of the goddess Nike, and in his left hand a scepter inlaid with jewels with an eagle perched atop it. The throne, decorated with gold, precious stones, ebony, and ivory on the sides and on the foot mat, depicted mythological themes, scenes, paintings, frescoes, and engravings, mostly depicting Zeus's many victories.

Let's celebrate the victory in the temple!

The temple was magnificent. It was more than 90 feet long, its exterior columns positioned in a six-by-thirteen arrangement. The columns themselves were colossal, stretching up to 35 feet high. The interior consisted of three parts: the *pronaos*, the front porch where the winners of the Olympic Games were given wreaths; the *opisthodomos* at the back of the building; and the actual sanctuary where the god Zeus was placed. Athletes from all over Greece competed in the games, each of them wanting to do their best. The games followed strict rules and athletes who broke them were punished.

AEGEAN SEA

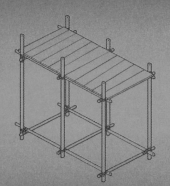

Scaffolding

Wooden poles and boards were joined by ropes to facilitate working at considerable heights.

One person cannot manage it

Not only sculptors, but also goldsmiths, carpenters, carvers, ironmongers, painters, and metal engravers all worked on the sculpture. According to legend, the sons of the sculptor Phidias also had their share in the birth of the statue. They had the special privilege of cleaning dirt from the statue.

Gold & ivory

Ivory was shaped and bent with water vapor. It was created by heating water in a huge bronze cauldron, while smaller pieces were heated above a small cauldron. Gold was used in the form of thin slices. The slices were inserted into the clay molds. Smaller details were embossed by hand, while larger details used lead patterns.

Slowly but surely!

Initially, a smaller model of the statue was made of cheap material, then enlarged to the correct proportions, and the wooden core of the statue was made. Clay molds were then cast to produce the expensive parts. They were apparently numbered and gradually assembled into a whole. After approval, the statue had to be disassembled, transferred to the temple, reassembled, and the finishing touches could then begin.

Pool of oil

The statue stood in front of a pool of oil. The reason was simple: to help maintain a moist atmosphere and impede any cracking of the ivory pieces. It was consequently extremely easy to scoop some oil from the olive pool, coat the cracked parts, and pour the excess oil back. And was anything more beautiful than watching the reflection of the divine giant at night in the light of many lanterns and torches in a dark mirror?

ORIGINAL MODELS

IVORY SHAPING

ELEPHANT TUSKS

STATUE OF
THE GODDESS
NIKE

METAL
ENGRAVERS

IVORY
PLATES

The best sculptor

The creator of the statue of Zeus is one of the most important Greek artists of the time after the Greek-Persian wars, Phidias of Athens (490–430 BCE). He was not only a sculptor, but also a painter, architect, and engineer. He created bronze statues of Apollo and Athena, and participated in the realization of the Parthenon temple. He became immortal, however, thanks to the statue of Zeus for the temple at Olympia, which he worked on for several years. The invitation to work in Olympia also saved him from some difficulties.

FINE OLYMPIAN COIN

Phidias's workshop

An excavation in Olympia in the 1950s revealed a workshop with the remains of a junkyard with the very materials and tools used to construct the statue. The bowl that belonged to Phidias also lay there. It is of interest that this workshop was not destroyed like the others after the work was finished; on the contrary, an altar of the gods was set up there. The inscription on the bottom of the teapot confirms clearly to whom it belonged: "*Feidiu eimi*—I belong to Phidias." Extraordinary people from the past obviously needed quite ordinary things, just as we do. And, like us, they cared very much about them.

The main part

Transporting the cast and numbered parts was extremely important: Imagine losing the tiniest one! Everything would have to start from the beginning and the whole work would be lost. It was a real test of patience and discipline: assemble, number, disassemble. Then you had to transport everything and not lose anything on the way! Then reassemble everything all over again. Then, the last and most challenging part began: completion.

The ivory

The ivory came from elephant tusks and hippopotamus teeth. In modern times the material used for the statue would cost around $22 million dollars!

PHIDIAS'S WORKSHOP

No work was done without tools!

The tools for making the statue included an anvil, a hammer, a spatula, diggers, trowels, chisels, and ancient drills. The discovery in the 1950s of a well-preserved rectangular ground plan indicated that there was a workshop near the temple. Tools, a bronze cauldron, the remains of gold, ivory, semi-precious stones, and glass were also found there.

Oh Zeus, what is the truth?

There are two stories about the destruction of the statue. The first involves a fire in either in 408 or 475 CE. The second states that the statue was destroyed by angry Christians when they ravaged the pagan idols. Neither can be confirmed with any certainty. We do know, however, that this is the last significant work of Phidias, because shortly after it was placed in the temple in 433 BCE, he died.

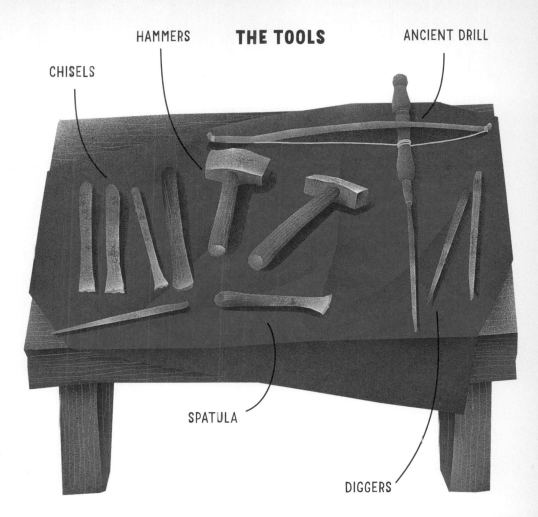

HAMMERS · **THE TOOLS** · ANCIENT DRILL

CHISELS

SPATULA

DIGGERS

SALVADOR DALÍ

Zeus as inspiration

The Statue of Zeus inspired many artists; Salvador Dalí, for example, created a monumental painting in 1954. In the first half of the 18th century, Horatio Greenough created a statue called "Zeus the Legislator," which took him eight whole years to make. The mythological scenes, the sphinx, and the other decorative elements of the chair on which Zeus rested have been the subject of countless reconstructions attempted by masters and artists throughout history.

The Temple of Artemis at Ephesus

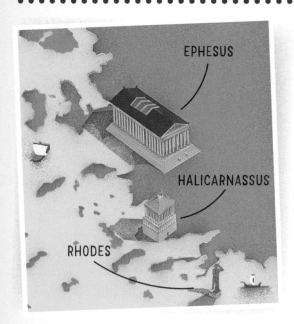

"The Temple of Artemis at Ephesus is the only house of the gods. Whoever looks will be convinced that a change of place has occurred: that the heavenly world of immortality has been placed on earth." With these words, Philo of Byzantium described this wonder of the world. And it is not an exaggeration. The temple, which was constructed over the period of a century, was truly magnificent and spectacular.

A place for the gods!

The temple was located in Ephesus, the iconic city of Asia Minor, in the area of what was then Anatolia (modern-day Turkey). It was a port and a center of trade and culture. A place where ships from many different countries, both near and far, arrived, unloaded, and loaded in ports. The colorful markets were bustling with activity.

Before this wonder

The Temple of Artemis had its predecessor, called "the Temple of Croesus." It was built before 546 BCE. The chief architect was Chersiphron, who built it with the support of King Croesus, who had conquered Ephesus shortly before construction began. According to preserved sources, it took 120 years to complete and was destroyed in 356 BCE by a man named Herostratus in an act of arson. The stone resisted the fire but the temple had wooden roof-beams that burned as swiftly as kindling.

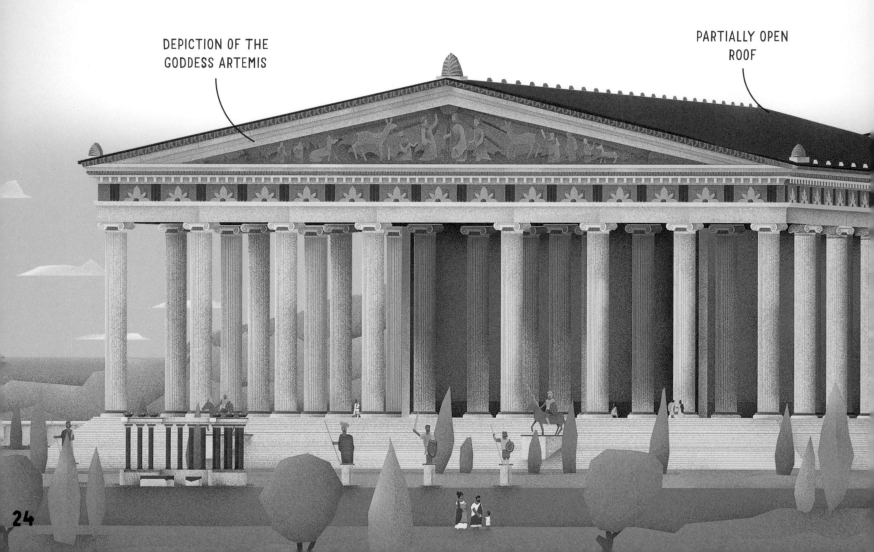

DEPICTION OF THE GODDESS ARTEMIS

PARTIALLY OPEN ROOF

Who will pay for it?

Alexander the Great, who ruled Ephesus in 334 BCE, presented the high priest of the temple with a generous offer: financing the construction and taking over the patronage in exchange for a small counter-service—carving his name into the stones of the temple. The Ephesians, however, tactfully refused. Even the gods at that time had certain conflicts of interest.

Our goddess, our money

The citizens of the city organized public funds, sold the valuable remains of the previous temple, and received contributions and donations from various sources. It is said that many women sold their valuable jewelry without hesitation. It is truly remarkable that the needed financial costs were finally secured, in part, through this early form of crowdfunding.

A dignified successor

On the site of the original ruined temple grew the classical Temple of Artemis, which was praised for its magnificence and monumentality even more than the previous one. As chief architect, Dinocrates of Rhodes supervised the construction of the temple. He was greatly assisted by the local architects Paeon and Demetrius. Being an architect for such a project meant putting your whole heart into it. But how long is a human life compared to a wonder of the world?

What type of material?

Building materials for the temple were wood and especially marble. Wagons were used to transport the heavy marble pieces. Parts of logs were used as axles between two wheels, with the shafts moving in an artificial wooden structure as a cylinder. The wagons were ox-driven.

A solid foundation is the law!

The builders chose swampy soil to reduce the impact of earthquakes, so they had to choose a massive foundation. According to the historical record they used, for example, compacted charcoal, on top of which they layered sheep fleece for isolation purposes. Then they could proceed with the confidence that the work was going well.

We think about everything!

The architect of the temple was very intelligent, anticipating, for example, the risk of flooding. So the base of the temple consisted of a marble staircase. Many innovative processes were used during the construction. It definitely involved costly, thoughtful, and demanding organization. The temple was practical yet monumental and at the same time gave the impression of touching the heavens. Its roof was partially open and made of roof tiles.

THE COLUMNS WERE BUILT PIECEMEAL

SWAMPY SUBSOIL

THE MARBLE STAIRS PROTECTED THE TEMPLE FROM FLOODING

Gradually but steadily

The construction of the Temple of Artemis was divided into several stages. The first small temple, built during the 7th century BCE, was gradually, up to the beginning of the 6th century BCE, extended by two more temples. Two other temples followed, referred to as the archaic (older) and classical (younger) Temple of Artemis.

Pulley

Using wheels and ropes, workers were able to lift heavy materials.

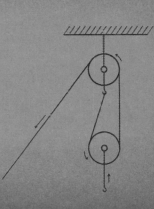

Legend

Where to get a huge amount of precious marble? According to legend, a young shepherd named Pixodar found an area suitable for marble extraction while grazing sheep.

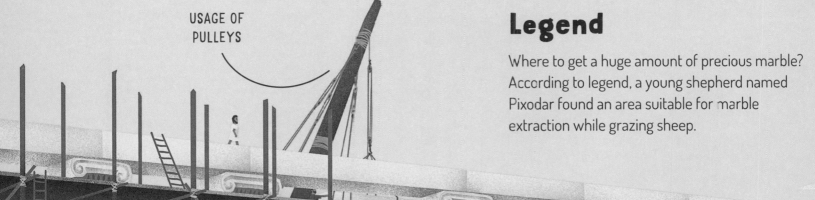

USAGE OF PULLEYS

WHEELS FACILITATE MATERIAL TRANSFER

RAMP

A magnificent goddess

Thus, in a dignified and magnificent temple, a statue made from the most precious materials was built. It glittered from a distance with gold, silver, and precious stones. The base was of extremely rare ebony wood. There was no doubt that the city of Ephesus had the powerful protection of a noble goddess whom everyone had to respect. The statue showed Greek and Eastern artistic elements and was revered the world over for its intercultural character.

BEES AS A SIGN
OF PRIESTS

A temple—a place for gods, festivals, and money

Religious events, celebrations, and sacrifices were not the only functions conducted at the temple. It was an important social center as well, since at that time both areas were closely interconnected. Significant events, decisions, feasts, and festivities could not take place without religious ceremonies and rituals. Likewise, the temple functioned as an economic center, bank, and mint. Last but not least, it was a shelter for the needy, a place guaranteeing the right of asylum.

Cult of the goddess

She would not be a goddess if her honors were not shrouded in wonderful mythological secrets. According to legend Artemis and her brother, the god Apollo, were born in Ephesus. This is why Artemis was honored as the patron saint of the city and the goddess of the Ephesians. In addition to being the goddess of hunting, wild nature, wildlife, and fertility, she also enjoyed the privileged right of providing protection and asylum to those at risk. Pilgrims from lands far and wide—Greece, Anatolia, Palestine, Egypt, and Persia—came to see her.

GOTHS

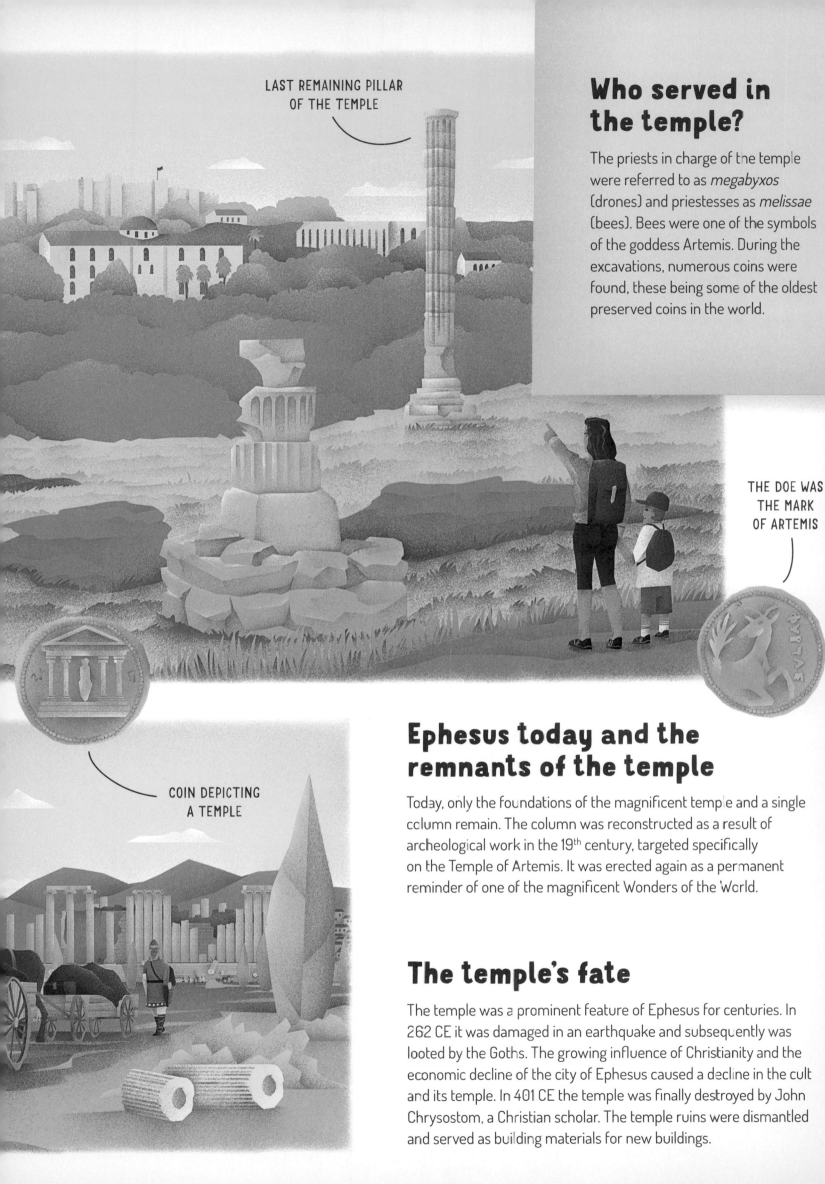

LAST REMAINING PILLAR OF THE TEMPLE

Who served in the temple?

The priests in charge of the temple were referred to as *megabyxos* (drones) and priestesses as *melissae* (bees). Bees were one of the symbols of the goddess Artemis. During the excavations, numerous coins were found, these being some of the oldest preserved coins in the world.

THE DOE WAS THE MARK OF ARTEMIS

COIN DEPICTING A TEMPLE

Ephesus today and the remnants of the temple

Today, only the foundations of the magnificent temple and a single column remain. The column was reconstructed as a result of archeological work in the 19th century, targeted specifically on the Temple of Artemis. It was erected again as a permanent reminder of one of the magnificent Wonders of the World.

The temple's fate

The temple was a prominent feature of Ephesus for centuries. In 262 CE it was damaged in an earthquake and subsequently was looted by the Goths. The growing influence of Christianity and the economic decline of the city of Ephesus caused a decline in the cult and its temple. In 401 CE the temple was finally destroyed by John Chrysostom, a Christian scholar. The temple ruins were dismantled and served as building materials for new buildings.

The Mausoleum at Halicarnassus

Mausolus II was a distinguished Persian ruler born in Milas, the capital of Caria. During his reign (377–353 BCE), he moved the capital to the coastal city of Halicarnassus. He thus became the city's founder and restorer. He won imperishable glory and eternal memory by building the Mausoleum.

FOUR-HORSE CHARIOT

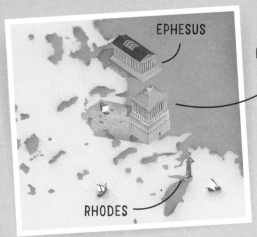

EPHESUS

HALICARNASSUS

RHODES

COLUMNS

The Mausoleum— What is it?

The ancient Mausoleum was a work of art. Due to the magnificence of the original structure, the term is used broadly today to describe the resting place of prominent people. The first one was a 150-foot-high rectangular marble tombstone. The base with the burial chamber measured about 60 feet and was surrounded by a colonnade of 36 columns. On top, there was a pyramid with 24 steps to the summit. The perfection and elaborateness with which it was built were beyond brilliant.

FRESCOES WITH SCENES OF BATTLES

UNPRECEDENTED NUMBER OF STATUES

A mysterious four-horse chariot

The top of the building was decorated with a four-horse chariot led by . . . Mausolus himself perhaps? Or maybe a Greek god? One cannot see that far, so it stretches our imagination. Whatever your theory is, it cannot be confirmed or disproven. Even today historians are clueless as to who actually drives the four-horse chariot.

Mausolus & Artemisia

His sister Artemisia, who was also his wife—family relationships were even more complicated back then—had a great influence on the preparation, planning, construction, and completion of the work. They loved each other deeply, passionately—and to death. The ruler didn't live to see the Mausoleum's final form, so his remains were buried in its unfinished construction site. Artemisia took over supervising the construction. She died two years after Mausolus and was buried next to him. Afterward, the construction of the Mausoleum was managed by other enthusiasts.

Halicarnassus? Where is it?

The name *Halicarnassus* sounds mysterious, don't you think? It is now called Bodrum and is located in Turkey. The Halicarnassus area used to be a place where various cultural influences of the ancient world met. Local Carian elements mixed with Eastern and Greek ones, the latter of which eventually prevailed. At its peak, Halicarnassus was a city full of mostly Greek elements, including the Mausoleum.

Crane

Large wheelers moved several pulleys to lift the heaviest loads to the required height.

COLUMN SHAFT

STATUES WERE LIFTED BY CRANES

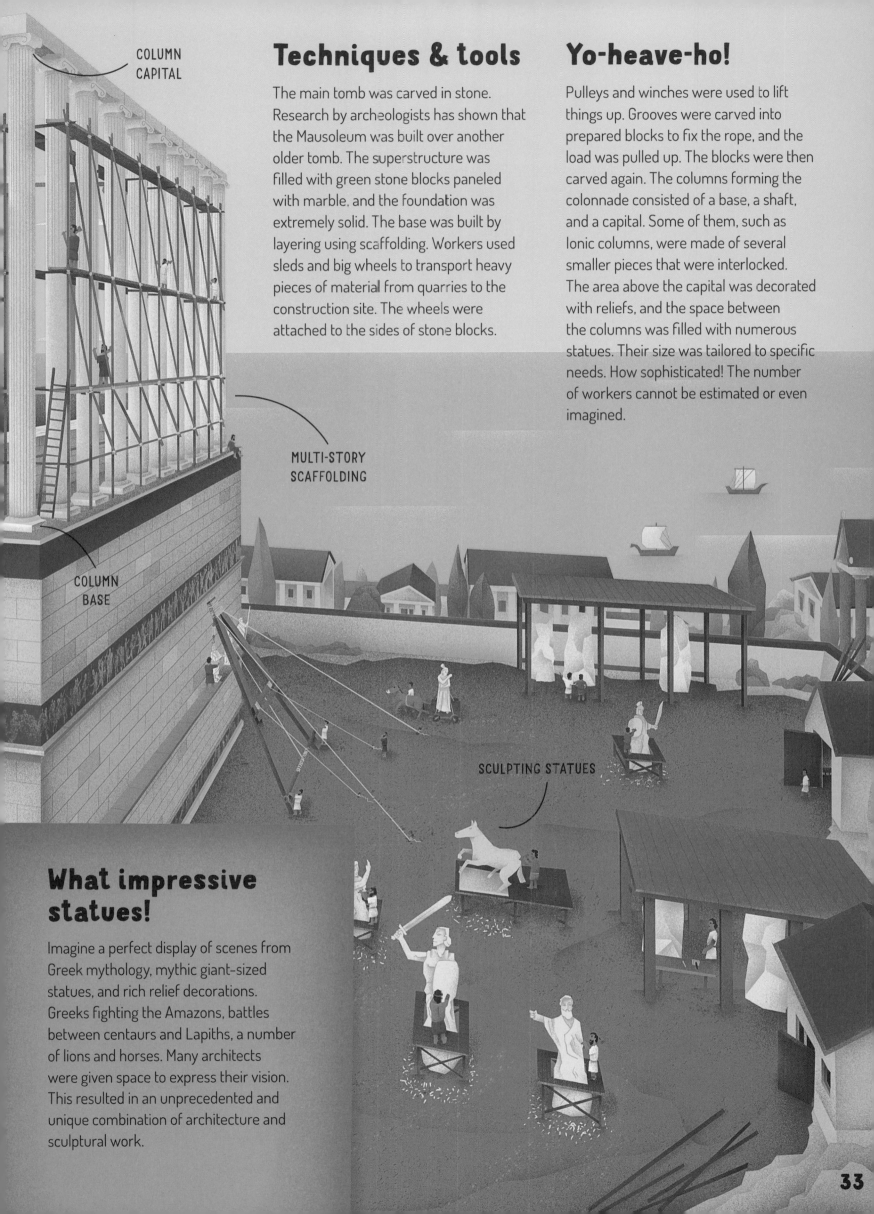

COLUMN
CAPITAL

Techniques & tools

The main tomb was carved in stone. Research by archeologists has shown that the Mausoleum was built over another older tomb. The superstructure was filled with green stone blocks paneled with marble, and the foundation was extremely solid. The base was built by layering using scaffolding. Workers used sleds and big wheels to transport heavy pieces of material from quarries to the construction site. The wheels were attached to the sides of stone blocks.

Yo-heave-ho!

Pulleys and winches were used to lift things up. Grooves were carved into prepared blocks to fix the rope, and the load was pulled up. The blocks were then carved again. The columns forming the colonnade consisted of a base, a shaft, and a capital. Some of them, such as Ionic columns, were made of several smaller pieces that were interlocked. The area above the capital was decorated with reliefs, and the space between the columns was filled with numerous statues. Their size was tailored to specific needs. How sophisticated! The number of workers cannot be estimated or even imagined.

MULTI-STORY
SCAFFOLDING

COLUMN
BASE

SCULPTING STATUES

What impressive statues!

Imagine a perfect display of scenes from Greek mythology, mythic giant-sized statues, and rich relief decorations. Greeks fighting the Amazons, battles between centaurs and Lapiths, a number of lions and horses. Many architects were given space to express their vision. This resulted in an unprecedented and unique combination of architecture and sculptural work.

Different influences, one unit

Uniquely, the Mausoleum combined several influences that were not combined elsewhere. Consider this: the roof is influenced by Egyptian architecture, the temple includes Greek elements, and the individual floors combine both. And we have not even touched on the diversity of the sculptures!

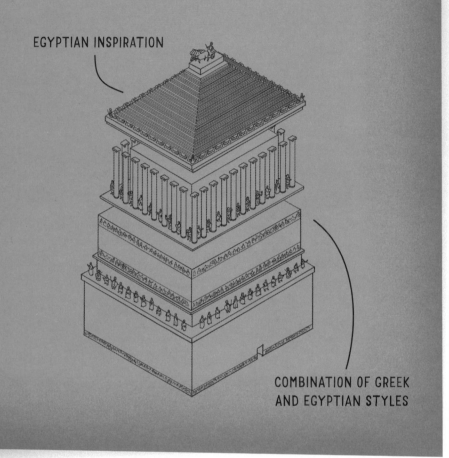

EGYPTIAN INSPIRATION

COMBINATION OF GREEK AND EGYPTIAN STYLES

The end of the mysterious tomb

The Mausoleum was destroyed by an earthquake in the 13th century. The solid stone blocks were used for other buildings in the area, such as the celebrated church of St. Peter and St. Paul. In the 19th century, archeologists discovered statues that had apparently originated from Bodrum. They immediately started excavating, hoping to find the remainder of the Mausoleum! After a tough beginning, their efforts were crowned with success. The rest of the building was found buried with fragments of horse and lion statues, human statues, and columns.

A KNIGHT OF MALTA

Where is the treasure?

No one knows what happened to the treasure from Mausolus's tomb. According to legend, it was either robbed by some of the Knights of Malta when they collected material for fortifications in 1522, or by pirates who learned about the great wealth hidden in the tomb. The tomb definitely contained gold, clothing, and jewelry until the 15th century. Archeologists, though, have only found mortal remains. Whoever used the valuables to make something of themselves, we will never know.

Construction and glory

The most renowned sculptors and artists aspired to work on this prestigious structure. And no wonder! It provided them with imperishable glory and power. The candidates included some highly renowned names: Pytheus created the building and the four-horse chariot. Other prominent architects worked on the four cardinal sides: Timotheus on the south side, Scopas on the east side, Bryaxis on the north side, and Leochares on the west side. The rectangular shape was highly advantageous; an oval—or any other shape— would not have allowed the art to be presented to all onlookers simultaneously.

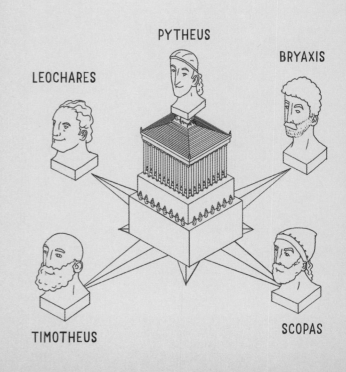

The influence of the Mausoleum

Like every extraordinary wonder, the Mausoleum influenced other rulers and big names. In the center of Alexandria, Alexander the Great built his tomb following the model of the Mausoleum. It also inspired the creator of the Taj Mahal in India, which was commissioned by the emperor Shah Jahan after he lost his beloved wife, as well as the creator of Castel Sant'Angelo, also known as the Mausoleum of Hadrian, which the Roman Emperor built for his family. One of the newer imitations of the Mauscleum is Lenin's Mausoleum in Moscow, Russia.

The Message of the Mausoleum

Power. Imperishable glory. Eternal memory. The desire for immortality. It is all inter-connected and united under the roof of a magnificent and monumental work that the world had never before seen. This was the vision of Mausolus II, which then became a reality. The Mausoleum is admired, revered, and inspiring. It is a wonder of the world, the mere memory of which makes us stand in awe. And that's the way it should be. It is further proof that the human spirit and art can win over death, at least for a while.

The Colossus of Rhodes

An impressive guy, huh? The Colossus of Rhodes was probably built between 292 and 280 BCE. The bronze statue of the god Helios was around 100 feet tall, with a 50-foot-high marble pedestal. Start counting! The statue was built over 12 years; each year it grew by less than 10 feet on average. In those days, sculptures were either carved from stone or cast from bronze. The Colossus of Rhodes, however, was an extraordinary statue; no one had ever tried to carve such a gigantic statue.

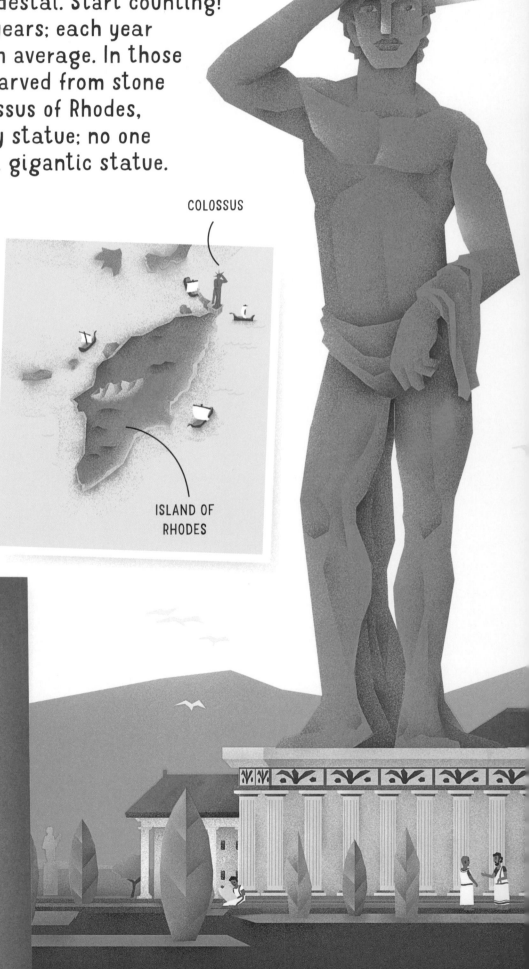

COLOSSUS

ISLAND OF RHODES

The Island of Rhodes

One of the 227 inhabited Greek islands in the Aegean Sea, it is strategically located between Asia Minor, Egypt, Syria-Palestine, and the Aegean region. It was a center of business, art, and public speaking. As it was renowned for having the most important sculpture schools, where else would you find better experts for such a building?

Take a look at the giant!

No exact description of this striking guy has been preserved, but we do have a few facts. The raised right hand, shielding Helios's eyes, was attached to his head for stability. The statue was likely naked, wearing a cloth at most. He had a gilded crown on his head and one leg forward. In this way he resisted the onslaught of the wind and earthquakes. He seemed like he had a great deal on his mind.

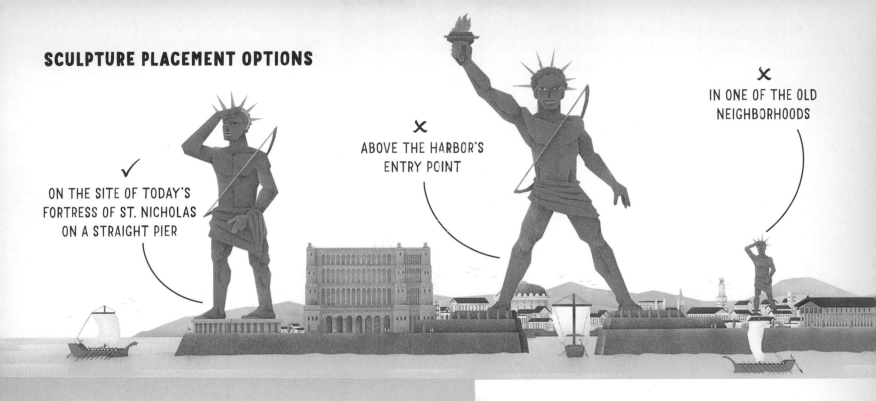

✓ ON THE SITE OF TODAY'S FORTRESS OF ST. NICHOLAS ON A STRAIGHT PIER

✗ ABOVE THE HARBOR'S ENTRY POINT

✗ IN ONE OF THE OLD NEIGHBORHOODS

Chares of Lindos

This famous sculptor is the creator of the Colossus of Rhodes. He might look inconspicuous, but he was a well-known student of the even more celebrated and world-famous Lysippos. His reputation preceded him! The construction of the statue of the god Helios provided him with glory and immortality during his lifetime. Chares left nothing to chance. He first created the individual parts of the statue on a small model, and then enlarged and fine-tuned the proportions. Next he just had to choose the right place . . .

Where should I put the Colossus?

"Are you guys crazy?!" Chares said to the townspeople, who thought they knew best where the statue should be built. "The colossus cannot straddle the entrance to the harbor. If it were to collapse, it would destroy the city—and you in it. No, I won't be responsible for this!" And his anger paid off. Common sense prevailed and he won the dispute. In accordance with his vision, the statue was built not straddling the harbor, nor inland in an old neighborhood, but on a pier.

So much bronze!

According to classical sources, it took nearly 20 tons of bronze and over 10 tons of iron to build the statue of the Colossus of Rhodes, which was about 20 to 30 tons! Although only the external surface of the statue (the "skin") was bronze, it was said to have caused a shortage of bronze throughout the ancient world during its construction. And inside? Iron and stone. During its construction, 8 tons of iron were used. In short, tons and tons of iron, stone, and rivets.

CHARES'S SCULPTURE SCHOOL IN THE CITY

Building the Colossus

Bronze, stone, and iron. Those were the main materials needed for the giant. Just imagine! A bronze cube with sides approximately one foot long weighed the same as three well-fed grown men. The Colossus had to be well reinforced, so his calves were filled with huge stone blocks. What a big dude! As such, the statue was not built at once. At its heel, there was a workshop in which the individual parts were divided and shaped. Then, the plates were joined together by rivets through prepared holes. A great, huge, and well-thought-out building kit.

Ramps!

Stones and gravel were placed around the sculpture so that the workers could transport the individual parts to the dedicated location. The workers built long ramps, which covered all sides of the Colossus. Thus, it was possible to advance to the upper floors and cleverly solidify the existing part of the statue.

MODEL OF THE SCULPTURE

Lost-wax casting technique

The various parts of the statue were made by encasing temporary wax models in clay. The entire assemblage was fired, causing the original wax to melt away. Lastly, liquid metal was poured into the empty mold. Piece by piece, the statue was created this way.

IRON CONSTRUCTION
INSIDE THE SCULPTURE

CRANES

SCAFFOLDING

SPIRAL RAMP

Rivets!

Small but very important pins reinforced the entire building.

LIGHTER MATERIALS
CARRIED BY DONKEYS

MATERIALS CARRIED
BY OXEN

Helios on the move

According to mythology, when the gods divided the earth among them, Helios was riding his sun carriage gracefully across the sky, and when he arrived, he was too late. The land was scattered far and wide. Smiling and without blinking, he drew out the island of Rhodes from the depths of the sea and lit it up with his brightness. Not a single muscle shook in his muscular body. And so the god Helios belongs to the island of Rhodes—just as the rainbow belongs to the sky.

Can we do it?

When the inhabitants of the island fought off the invasion of Demetrius Poliorcetes in 304 BCE, they sold their siege machines. Well done! They received over 10 tons of silver. With this kind of capital, it was a good idea to begin the construction of a Wonder of the World, don't you think?

SIEGE MACHINE

Kolossoi

Originally, *kolossoi* was the term for wax figures and dolls used for magical rituals. Today, *colossus* represents something huge, going beyond the normal dimensions.

I can do it!

Not even the tallest and strongest man could hug a single finger of the Rhodes giant. After all, each and every finger was cast from one piece of bronze and was taller than a man of average height. Sure, many people—old and young, big and small—might have tried, but none succeeded.

IT BROKE AT THE KNEES

The fall of the Rhodes giant

In 226 BCE, on a dark October night, the Colossus broke at the knees and collapsed. No wonder—the preceding earthquake left no stone unturned. The giant's hands and the golden crown disappeared first. The heaviest remains of the statue, which could not be removed, were beheld by many who came to admire the ruins of the Rhodes god for years to come.

Hope for recovery

Ptolemy III was an Egyptian monarch who offered to pay for the reconstruction of the statue. He wanted to provide over 10 tons of silver, 100 builders, and 350 helpers with a generous salary for the statue to be renovated. But there was a prophecy from Delphi claiming that if the statue was erected again, the sun god would be angry and punish the island of Rhodes and its inhabitants. Needless to say, these plans were abandoned.

What happened in the end?

In 653 CE, Muslim invaders disembarked in Rhodes, bringing more than 900 camels with them! They then disassembled the remains of the broken Colossus. It is said that the bronze they earned was melted and used to make coins, weapons, and tools. This is how the legendary Colossus of Rhodes came to an end.

The Lighthouse of Alexandria

It was more than 450 feet high, had three floors, distinct architectural features, and a number of sculptures. The floors had various shapes; the first one was square and the second one octagonal. The highest part of the lighthouse was cylindrical. An unknown god looked down from the top. It could have been Poseidon, the god of the sea; Helios, the god of the sun; Zeus, the savior; Ptolemy I; or perhaps the Egyptian goddess Isis. It might even have been a universal statue that was altered according to given circumstances to ensure the continuous operation of the lighthouse. How convenient!

LIKELY
A REMOVABLE STATUE

FIRE IN AN OPEN
IRON BASKET

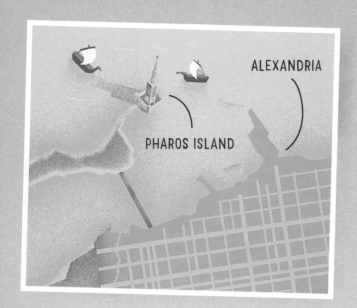

ALEXANDRIA

PHAROS ISLAND

The Ptolemaic dynasty

It was the longest-reigning dynasty in Egypt. Ptolemy I Soter, also known as the Savior, was a Macedonian general and a close friend of Alexander the Great. Despite their friendship, he assumed the title of king without further ado, after the collapse of Alexander's empire. He thus gained a rich and glorious empire, which he ruled with a firm hand and enlarged with many glorious buildings, including the renowned lighthouse.

Why here?

Alexandria, the city of fountains, gardens, luxury palaces, and temples. The center of Mediterranean trade, with its own harbor. Of all the Alexandrias founded by Alexander the Great, it is the most prominent one—and the only one that has survived into the present day. But what is it missing? A lighthouse! And what about a Wonder of the World? What about the nearby island? Pharos, or Faros in Greek, the site of the majestic Lighthouse of Alexandria, was within sight of the coast of Alexandria.

SOSTRATUS OF CNIDUS

DEXIFANES

Who is going to build the lighthouse?

Ptolemy appointed his good friend, Sostratus of Cnidus, as the lighthouse's architect. And his choice couldn't have been better! His father Dexifanes was one of the engineers and architects who first built Alexandria.

I swim, I win

In a battle with the Republicans, the Roman Emperor Julius Caesar jumped into the water near Alexandria clenching his magenta cloak in his teeth and holding valuable documents in his raised hand to prevent their getting wet. His dedication paid off, and he won. The parade organised by Caesar to celebrate the victory included the unveiling of a monumental lighthouse model. It even had a fire at the top. Historians do not say whether there were also mirrors.

JULIUS CAESAR

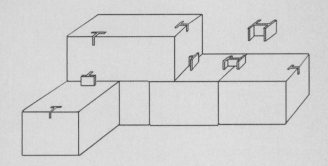

Reinforcement

Stone blocks of limestone and granite were drilled, fastened with metal hooks and clamps, and sealed with molten lead. This prevented the oxidation of the metal and guaranteed the tightness of the joints. What is surprising is that the stone blocks were laid dry!

Wooden frames?

Yes! Although the lighthouse stood on a rock, wood was essential. As the rock and soil were spread unevenly, a structure of wooden grids had to be built under the foundation. Guess which kind of trees were chopped down? Oaks. They are durable, solid, and water resistant.

Technique

There was a need to chisel away the rock and build an embankment. The foundation platform was bordered with stone blocks. The inner space was filled with granite blocks and sealed with a mortar mix. Several such layers formed a solid base that protected the lighthouse from waves and earthquakes.

MATERIALS DRAWN BY OXEN

A SURVEYING INSTRUMENT CALLED A GROMA

Hard work!

It took 20 years to build the lighthouse, as the work was arduous. The ancient workers who built the lighthouse, though, were not slaves—they got paid. The slaves worked in the quarries (and deserved to be compensated in gold, but no one thought of that back then).

A WINCH

A SIMPLE CRANE

Materials

The materials used to build the lighthouse included light limestone, reddish granite, bronze, marble, stone, and lead. In other words, *a lot* of limestone, granite, bronze, marble, stone, and lead. The granite was imported from quarries in Aswan, which was also where the pyramid builders went for their materials.

SCAFFOLDING

Wood as far as the eye can see

The fire was lit in an open lantern and was reportedly visible from over 30 miles. Fuel was transported up a spiral ramp using a lifting device, probably a hoist. Side rooms served as observations posts during the day.

Telescope

Yes, that's right! The ingeniously designed series of mirrors inside the lighthouse seem to have reflected and amplified the firelight, and it also helped the Alexandrians spot arriving boats, as the mirrors functioned like a telescope.

Ordinary mirrors?

Honestly, there was nothing ordinary about them. The mirrors were usually made of either glossy metal (bronze) or glass. But in the Lighthouse of Alexandria—and here's the catch—the mirrors were quite remarkable! Some claim that they were made of transparent stone, others that it was finely worked glass. Either way, the mirrors were still functional and impressive even when Egypt was conquered by Arabs in 642 CE.

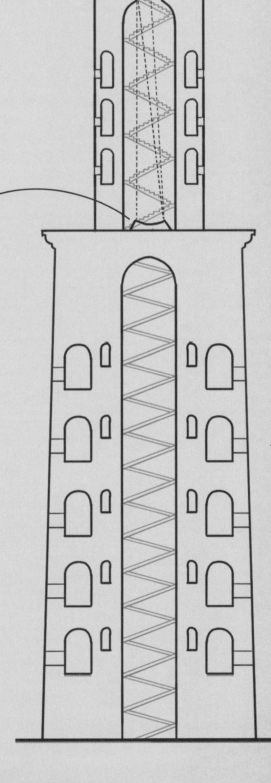

EYEPIECE

SECONDARY MIRROR

PRIMARY MIRROR

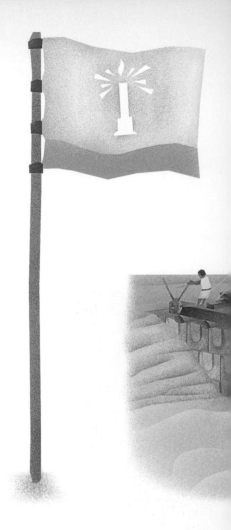

A symbol of Alexandria

For ages, the lighthouse symbolized Alexandria and the power of the ruler of Egypt. We could even say it served as a kind of banner advertising the city as a major tourist destination. But while the lighthouse no longer stands in Alexandria, it can still be found on the city flag.

ARABIC CITADEL OF QAITBAY

When the fire died

The lighthouse survived more than 20 major recorded earthquakes. In the 4th century, however, one earthquake put out the fire on the platform for good. The lighthouse was then used only during the day, as the mirrors—and, naturally, the bright facade of the building—reflected the daylight. Around 875 CE, a wooden dome was built atop the building. When a gust of wind tore the wooden structure down, a small mosque was constructed at the top instead.

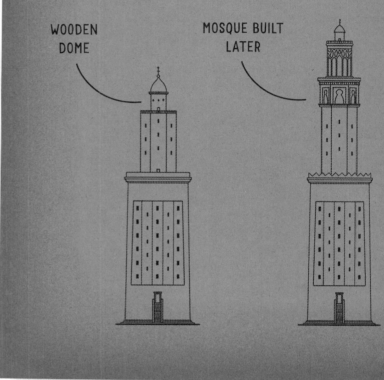

WOODEN DOME

MOSQUE BUILT LATER

How to build bulwarks & embankments?

The solution is quite ingenious: Push and tie wooden foundations together. Put reed baskets with clay between them. Form an embankment sloping to the sea, build a stone frame of the same height, fill the space between the embankment and the frame with sand, and erect a pillar. Let it dry, take down the frame, and wait until the embankment is undermined and the pillar collapses into the sea. Sound complicated? You're right. That's why they mostly used this other technique: boats were loaded with stone blocks and sunk in a designated spot.

How did it end?

In terms of architecture, the lighthouse can be seen as a forerunner of modern skyscrapers, which are everywhere nowadays but weren't thousands of years ago, making it all the more inspiring! It managed to maintain the reputation of one of the world's highest lighthouses for nearly 15 centuries! During that period, it withstood many earthquakes until one ill-fated earthquake razed it to the ground. The Arab fort Qaitbay was built on the original site in 1477.

© B4U Publishing for Albatros,
an imprint of Albatros Media Group, 2021.
5. května 1746/22, Prague 4, Czech Republic
Author: Ludmila Hénková
Illustrator: Tomáš Svoboda
Printed in China by Leo Paper Group.
ISBN: 978-80-00-06134-4

www.albatrosbooks.com

albatros_books_   Albatros Books   Albatros Books US